HIGH ON

NEW YORK

PHOTOGRAPHS BY PETER B. KAPLAN

INTRODUCTION BY PAUL GOLDBERGER

CAPTIONS BY THOMAS E. NORTON AND PETER B. KAPLAN

HARRY N. ABRAMS, INC.

PUBLISHERS NEW YORK

To Eddie Nelkin, an old and dear friend who is no more...he now sees these views everyday.

To my parents, Chet and Bill, and to my dear wife, Sharon; without their support none of this would have been possible.

Project Director: Robert Morton

Editor: Ruth Peltason

Designer: Dirk Luykx

Library of Congress Cataloging-in-Publication Data
Kaplan, Peter B.
    High on New York.
    1. Photography, Artistic. 2. New York (N.Y.)—
Description—Views. 3. Kaplan, Peter B.
I. Goldberger, Paul. II. Norton, Thomas E. III. Title.
TR654.K358   1986   779'.997471043   85–20085
ISBN 0–8109–1095–0

All photographs taken of or from the Chrysler Building
courtesy of, and with special thanks to, Mr. Jack Kent Cooke,
owner

Published in 1986 by Harry N. Abrams, Incorporated, New
York. All rights reserved. No part of the contents of this
book may be reproduced without the written permission of
the publishers

Printed and bound in Japan

1: This photograph was made in 1982, well before the restoration work had begun in preparation for the Statue of Liberty's centennial in 1986.

"For years I tried to get permission to climb inside the arm of the statue in order to photograph from the rim of the torch, but all my requests were turned down; the arm has been closed to the public since 1916. However, when I began working as the 'preferred photographer' for the Statue of Liberty—Ellis Island Foundation, I received the necessary go-aheads from the National Park Service and up I went.

"I've made lots of climbs to the top of the statue since then, but I will always remember one evening in particular when I was up in the torch and heard the strains of 'God Bless America' sung by a boatload of Circle Line passengers, as they passed by Liberty Island three hundred feet below—I had goose bumps all over."

2–3: July 4th, 1982—a spectacular display of fireworks on a perfect summer evening provides a made-to-order opportunity for a portrait of lower New York as seen from the top of the Manhattan Bridge. The white lines in the sky were caused by planes overhead.

4–5: The skyline of midtown Manhattan as photographed from a helicopter at sunrise, the scene dominated by the United Nations Secretariat Building reflected in the East River.

This thirty-nine-story tower was New York's first "curtain wall" building, designed by Wallace K. Harrison working with an international committee in 1952 on a site that was formerly occupied by cattle yards and abattoirs.

8: "A few years ago, after the volcanic eruptions at Mt. St. Helens in Oregon, I was commissioned by Life magazine to take a series of photographs of sunrises and sunsets from the top of the Empire State Building. The purpose of this exercise was to record what effects, if any, there would be in the earth's atmosphere from the spreading cloud of volcanic dust as it floated eastward. A century ago, after the eruption of Mt. Krakatoa in Indonesia, sunsets became more vivid in color for several years. This didn't happen in 1980, but the photograph of the Chrysler Building's spire, with the bridges over Hell Gate in the distance, is nonetheless pretty spectacular."

C O N T E N T S

INTRODUCTION

by Paul Goldberger

THE CLASSIC VIEW OF THE NEW YORK SKYLINE IS OF SOMETHING FAR off and untouchable. It is exquisite, and glimmers with the sparkle of temptation, but even as it attracts us it seems to keep us at a distance. This kind of skyline is an object to be looked at, a thing to inspire awe. It is not something that encourages intimacy at all.

Altogether different are the photographs of Peter B. Kaplan. The New York skyline that he shows us is something as alive, as breathing, as a photograph of a child, or an animal, or a rare flowering plant, and he brings us right into the middle of it. It is no accident that Peter B. Kaplan began his career as a nature photographer, for he approaches the city in the same way—stealthily, seeking a closeness that is normally barred to those of his breed.

These photographs are a celebration of height, of New York's love for it, and of Kaplan's remarkable ability to achieve it. But for all one has to be astonished by his photographic method—his willingness to climb high with the steelworkers, higher still with the men who change the flashing lights atop the antennas—getting to the top of things is not the essence of Peter B. Kaplan's work. It is what he is most famous for, of course, but in truth the skyscraper is not his Mount Everest, there merely to be scaled. He climbs it not just to reach the top, or even to shoot photographs down from the top. He is more like a naturalist who studies the flora and fauna of mountaintops, who climbs high so as to be able to dig deep and understand certain things we cannot grasp from the ground.

9

It is all clear from the pictures themselves. When Peter B. Kaplan reaches the top of a skyscraper, he does not just shoot down, although he surely does some of that, and he does not just shoot across the city. He prowls in the nooks and crannies, he discovers details, he looks at the people who are up there with him, and he keeps moving. For Kaplan the skyline is a vast jungle gym, something to be climbed up and around and through and over. In this sense he could not be more different from his friend, the late photographer Ruth Orkin, whose classic books recorded the passage of New York, and of nature, before her window on Central Park West. Where Ruth Orkin let her vantage point be static—creating a deliberately ironic juxtaposition to the constantly changing subject matter she photographed—Peter B. Kaplan seems never to sit still. He changes position constantly, looking at the city from every angle; his city is never a tableau, never a neatly framed composition. Like every talented photographer, he is making compositions. But it is in making us feel the tactile sense of this city, in making us feel that we, too, are climbing and touching this extraordinary object that is New York, that Peter B. Kaplan excels.

This makes Peter B. Kaplan an ideal photographer for New York at this moment. The city is probably the object of more romantic affection now than it has been at any time since the 1930s, and Kaplan surely grasps this—indeed, in some of his nighttime views of the entire skyline, including the spectacular shot showing fireworks bursting over the East River, the Brooklyn Bridge, and the Manhattan skyline, he plays the current weakness for New York's romantic imagery to the hilt. So, too, with Kaplan's fondness for photographing restoration of the ornate details of the city's landmarks: it reminds us that these buildings are no longer dismissed as quaint eccentricities, but are now considered essential parts of the cityscape.

Kaplan does not document very thoroughly the new generation of romantic skyscrapers, buildings like AT&T and Trump Tower, that have broken architecture out of the grip of the International Style. There are glimpses of these buildings here, but Kaplan is less interested in recording architecture than he is in giving us a broader, more interpretive sense of the city's imagery. He is committed to showing us a city in process, a city that is growing and changing now as much as it ever has. We do not feel in these photographs a direct sense of the pain that this sometimes causes—there are no pictures of beloved buildings being torn down, no photographs that stand as polemics against the overbuilding and overcrowding that are making Manhattan so much more difficult a place than it has ever been. But in a less pointed way Peter B. Kaplan speaks to these issues, for it is clear from these photographs that his city is not a fixed object; it is a place always in motion, ever-changing, a place in which energy and light are the constants more than brick and stone.

Consistent with this is Kaplan's preference for showing us bits and pieces, parts of buildings instead of wholes, and single buildings instead of huge cityscapes, which makes us feel the city as a collection of parts far more than the classic skyline views, which portray a falsely neat and pat totality. But Kaplan also shows us more literally the incompleteness of the city, with an occasional glimpse at buildings under construction, as well as frequent looks at the people who build the new generation of skyscrapers—workers whose careers he documents with a healthy respect.

The photographs of construction workers are something of a Peter B. Kaplan trademark, as much as his signature shots that look straight down the sides of skyscrapers. Not since Lewis Hine, surely, has anyone paid as much attention to the people who have actually built the skyline as Peter B. Kaplan has. He is an empathetic photographer—he shoots only what he feels a sense of camaraderie with—and if that is true of the buildings he documents, it is all the more true of his photographs of the workers. It is not merely his willingness to climb high and take the same risks they do that makes the workers comfortable with him and he with them, and neither is it his gruff voice and his casual manner, though it is no surprise that they like his style more than they would that of the fashion photographer fussing endlessly with lights and props. Kaplan is a kind of blend of roughness and mellowness, like a Hell's Angel who has settled in Big Sur, and he could not be more different from most urban photographers.

The city is a backdrop for human activity in these pictures; it is ever-present, but there is a drama going on in the foreground, and that is the lives of these people themselves. The pictures of construction workers range from the painters of the Queensboro Bridge to the steelworkers erecting skyscraper skeletons to the restorers fixing the delicate Gothic finials of St. Patrick's Cathedral. Unlike Lewis Hine, Peter B. Kaplan has no sociological purpose, save to remind us of the diversity of situations in which people can earn a living at such heights, and of the extent to which all of these extraordinary jobs are done by ordinary, living, breathing people, people to whom working a thousand feet above the street is as normal as working behind a lunch counter.

These photographs also give Kaplan a chance to reveal his compositional skill. The photograph of steelworkers atop the AT&T Building is a superb composition, with the men and the intersecting steel beams forming a powerful foreground, and the city below and the sky above joining to create a sumptuous yet deferential background. The composition here calls to mind not so much other photographs as the great prints of the 1920s by artists like Louis Lozowick, for the steel beams become lines of force, anchoring the composition. There is a hint, too, of the precisionist work of Sheeler here, though the presence of the workers, moving nimbly across the steel, makes it clear that this is a far cry from an industrial still life.

More romantic, surely, is the photograph of workers installing the antenna atop the World Trade Center, seventeen hundred feet above the street. What makes this remarkable is not simply the height, though one cannot but be somewhat awed by the fact that Peter B. Kaplan's camera is looking not up but down on these workers. The truly stunning thing is the clouds, which almost, but not quite, envelop the workers; the men appear to be floating in a white mist, so high up that at first glance they do not appear to be atop the skyline at all, but merely enveloped in haze. What connects them to the reality of the city is a wonderful punctuation mark, a tiny piece of the crown of the Woolworth Building poking through the clouds.

But more important than any of these things is the fact that the construction workers who specialize in working at these heights know that Kaplan understands their secret, which is that the world high above the city has an extraordinary magic, a tranquility that is very much its own. Here it is impossible not to remember once again that Peter B. Kaplan began his career as a nature photographer, for he looks to the city for much the same kind of escape—it is still a kind of wilderness, far away and private, that he seeks. He wants to be more like Ansel Adams than he will let on; one senses that he works in the city so as to be able to make of it something else—so as to be able to transcend it. It is telling to hear this photographer, whose work is so intimately connected with the pace and energy of the city, speak of climbing to the spire of the Empire State Building: "You get away from the filth and the noise and the overcrowding, and there is a kind of silence," Peter B. Kaplan said not long ago. "That is what I love about it. Where can you go in New York that is that far away from people? But when you get up on top of these structures—it is my very own urban wilderness."

Perhaps the most appealing aspect of Kaplan's style as a photographer is a kind of paradox in that he achieves the escape he seeks not by physical distance, but by closeness, even intimacy, with the things he photographs. He may be far away from the ground, but he is right on top of the spires, the bridge cables, the cornices, and the columns he photographs, and his photographs caress them. And what connotes escape for Peter B. Kaplan in the act of making pictures results in something else altogether for the rest of us, who are brought by these photographs right to the essence of their subject. These are no-nonsense pictures, going to the heart of the matter, yet the view they bring us is always fresh, and not only for the awareness of height that they engender.

We can feel this especially when he turns to buildings that are familiar, like the Chrysler Building, where the closeness of his camera to the subject brings a set of views that transcend the clichés. It is not easy to look in a new way at the Chrysler Building, but when Kaplan photographs the top of the tower with its special lighting, the entire building seems to glow as the architect William Van Alen would have had it. That picture zeroes in on the great profile of the Chrysler, including it for the record and freeing Kaplan, in a sense, to move on to views that are even more his own, like the shot down the side of the tower that shows us the famous hood-ornament gargoyle from above instead of below, as it is usually photographed; or the view of the very top of the spire at sunrise, with the arched crown barely visible below; or the shot that focuses on a portion of the arched crown, turning it into a piece of abstract sculpture.

There is also a view of the Chrysler Building and the Empire State Building, shot from an angle from which all other towers disappear, and these two, perhaps the most celebrated skyscraper silhouettes ever created, seem to stand together in conversation. It is one of the simplest photographs in the book, yet one of the most remarkable, for it makes of these two buildings, often compared but rarely juxtaposed, a world of their own. They stand chaste, proud, handsome, self-assured, like people more than buildings, and we feel looking at them here that the rest of the world has no relevance at all. Indeed, looking at this photograph is less like looking at two buildings as it is like catching two celebrated persons who are rarely seen together, as if a photo had been found of Le Corbusier conversing with Frank Lloyd Wright, or Picasso with Matisse.

The Empire State Building itself—so beloved to Peter B. Kaplan that he arranged to be married there, on a steel platform near the ninety-second floor with his guests assembled on the eighty-sixth floor public observatory below—seems, surprisingly, to come off best in his work when it is shot in tandem with other buildings, as in the Chrysler picture. The shot of the building at nightfall, its profile illuminated and the ornately lit Con Edison and Metropolitan Life towers before it, is a fine composition, glowing with the magic of evening light. But some of the other views of the Empire State have a touch of the razzle-dazzle to them, like the shots straight down the side of the building, or the view of the building with lasers shooting off the top, or the close-up of the tower top illuminated in red, looking like a part of the set for *Star Wars*. These are all spectacular, but they lack the subtlety of the best pictures in this book.

Peter B. Kaplan cannot make the World Trade Center beautiful, but he does manage to make it enticing as an object—in one case by catching it at just the moment when the sun turns it a rich pinkish orange, in another by looking down between the two towers. Here, perhaps for the first time, his specialty view looking straight down the side of a building (a shot he gets by sticking his camera onto a pole that is projected off the side of the roof) makes great sense, in large part because it turns the towers into two parts of an abstract composition, and we feel them play off against each other.

For the American Telephone and Telegraph building on Madison Avenue, the controversial "Chippendale skyscraper" by Philip Johnson and John Burgee, Kaplan positions himself right in the middle of the infamous broken pediment. And why not? It is just where everyone wants to be when they look at that building, and he makes us feel that swooping cutout, which here looks more like a tunnel than a building-top, in a way that no other photographer has managed to do. For the Woolworth Building, Cass Gilbert's lyrical, Mozartian tower of 1913, Kaplan once again focuses on a part and does not attempt to follow other photographers and shoot the whole; we see a close-up of the Gothic tracery that forms part of the crown, with the blue sky shining through, and that remarkable mix of delicacy and strength that Gilbert's design possesses is made instantly clear.

The offbeat sensibility that leads Kaplan to climb into the middle of the tops of buildings like AT&T and Woolworth also yields some splendid results when he moves away from skyscrapers. The Alice in Wonderland statue in Central Park seems at once mysterious and intimate when we look down on it, as we do here, though from an un-Kaplanesque low height. Too, we look down at the celebrated globe in the lobby of the New York Daily News Building, and—in one of the most spectacular photographs in the book—down on an airplane flying over Manhattan. And of course Peter B. Kaplan shoots the Thanksgiving Day parade, celebrated for its massive balloons, from above rather than from below, so that we not only look down on Superman in one view, in another we also feel with special intensity the great wall of buildings that defines a Manhattan street.

A number of these photographs, like the parade shot, redefine familiar spaces in the city. The best of these is surely the view of the interior of the great concourse of Grand Central Terminal, one of the city's triumphal rooms and almost invariably photographed from eye level. Kaplan swings high to give us a view that makes this space feel big and round and voluptuous; we feel the quality of the space, if not so completely the majesty of the architecture. And, oddly, the great room seems almost more intimate than it does in more conventional views. The view of the pedestrian bridge from the East Side of Manhattan to Ward's Island, looking straight down one of the towers, reinterprets this bridge as a purely abstract composition, while the view of Times Square at night, shot from on high, is among the few pictures taken in our time that makes this complex intersection feel like a true urban space. It is as matter-of-fact as any of Kaplan's pictures, but it brings us back completely to the age when Times Square was not only a visually spectacular thing, but a real place, a focal point for the life of the city.

So, too, with the Brooklyn Bridge, perhaps the hardest thing of all in New York to photograph with a fresh eye. As with the Chrysler Building, Peter B. Kaplan does a number of things, beginning with the almost conventional—in this case a view of one of the towers at night, cropped to fill the frame—and then going off on his own direction toward more abstract compositions. That first picture of the tower should not be sold short, however; it is a strong photograph, like the bridge itself at once dynamic and stable, possessing an ineffable mix of energy and repose. And letting the tower fill the frame makes us feel the tower as it is too rarely felt, as the city's greatest gateway.

And the bridge is, of course, the star of what must be the easiest photograph in this book to like, the view of fireworks bursting over the Manhattan skyline with the bridge in the foreground. As a type, this is not the kind of picture that only Peter B. Kaplan could make; it is a panorama, not a crisply focused shot from on high. But all the elements of Peter B. Kaplan's city are here. The composition is right, with the bridge and the buildings and the fireworks in perfect balance. The light is extraordinary, with the pink glow of the setting sun playing off just right against the fireworks, which give a shot of energy to the skyline. The city sparkles, it glows, it crackles; it is at once sumptuous and nimble in this picture. It is Peter B. Kaplan's gift to be able to render a New York that is not altogether real, and not altogether fantasy, but balanced tantalizingly, wonderfully, in between.

HIGH ON NEW YORK

THE PHOTOGRAPHS

One of New York's most delightful rooftops is that on
of the first tall buildings erected after the 1916 zoning

1981—the building was restored, regilded, and renamed the Crown Building.

18–19: "This photograph records a 'noble experiment' I attempted with the help of Mike Radigan, foreman of the crew working on the metalwork at the pinnacle of the Chrysler Building, during a massive restoration project.

"Our plan was to mount a pulley on the very tip of the spire so that we could hoist a camera there, while the scaffolding was still in place. That way I'd be able to take a progressive series of photographs as the scaffolds were removed, until, finally, nothing would stand in the way of a clear shot looking all the way down. Unfortunately, strong winds destroyed the apparatus we had so carefully contrived, so the 'ultimate' Chrysler Building photograph never materialized.

"Mike and I are visible at the base of the spire and below us are the roofs of the Chanin Building, the Commodore Hotel, and other tall structures in the neighborhood of Grand Central Terminal."

20–21: During the past twenty-five years, Sixth Avenue, or as it's officially titled, Avenue of the Americas, has been transformed from a rather shabby thoroughfare haunted by the elevated train that once rattled along its length, to an impressive, if somewhat sterile, canyon of corporate behemoths.

Here, looking south from the roof of the MGM Building at 55th Street, we see, from right to left, the New York Hilton Hotel, the headquarters of JC Penney, Equitable Life, Time & Life, Exxon, McGraw-Hill, and the Celanese Corporation. Further downtown, the sunlight struggles to pierce the haze.

22: "The Brooklyn Bridge is suspended from four massive cables anchored to its two stone towers. Only after I'd made dozens of climbs to the tops of the towers did I discover how to maneuver out beyond the inner cable to a position beneath the outer one, affording a clearer view of the Manhattan skyline directly in front of me."

23: The dark green polished granite IBM Building has dominated the intersection of Madison Avenue and 57th Street since it was completed in 1982. Designed by Edward Larrabee Barnes, its sleek surfaces contain vertical tracks for window-washing machines. This photograph was made looking straight down from inside one of these recesses, toward the traffic on Madison Avenue.

The result is a camera obscura effect: the surrounding buildings and street traffic are projected inside the shiny metal surface of the recessed track.

24–25: New York in an unusual portrait made on a hazy day, from the upper reaches of the Empire State Building. Air pollution, whatever negative things may be said about it, does produce some stunning atmospheric effects when photographed.

Even on a hazy day, some of the world's better known landmarks can be discerned—from Macy's to Bryant Park, to the RCA, Pan Am, and Chrysler buildings.

26: A view looking down and south from the top of the Empire State Building. Broadway veers diagonally across the New York street grid as it heads downtown from Herald Square at 34th Street toward Madison Square at 23rd Street.

    Visitors to the observation deck on the eighty-sixth floor gaze down toward 33rd Street, and the metal ornamentation that projects slightly beyond the stone exterior of the building can be seen directly beneath them. The world's third tallest building remains a favor-ite spot for tourists to visit and see for fifty miles in all directions.

27: Olympic Tower, designed by Skidmore, Owings & Merrill, caused quite a stir when built at Fifth Avenue and East 55th Street in 1974–76. This is a view of its south facade, photographed from one of the spires of its immediate downtown neighbor, St. Patrick's Cathedral.

    Way below is a cluster of three turn-of-the-century townhouses, now converted to commercial use, serving as reminders of an age when this area was exclusively residential.

28: "One day when we were photographing from a helicopter above midtown Manhattan, I looked down at Madison Avenue in the 40s and was struck by the bold graphic patterns of the scene: city buses in their specially marked lanes, cars, the terraced building. Sometimes the most surprising and memorable photographs just 'happen' when you least expect them."

29: Seen from high atop the IBM Building, these pedestrians walking on Madison Avenue near 57th Street resemble chess pieces on a board, their long shadows casting a surrealistic image.

30: This distinctive pink sidewalk was one of the original features of the office building at 270 Park Avenue erected for Union Carbide in 1976 by Skidmore, Owings

& Merrill. It has since been replaced by a more somber gray pavement, perhaps felt to be more appropriate for what is now the headquarters of Manufacturers-Hanover Trust Company.

31: Midtown Manhattan land values are so high and owners often so tenacious, that some unusual, even bizarre, arrangements have been worked out to accommodate a developer's failure to assemble an entire block for a building site.

In the case of 875 Third Avenue at the southeast corner of 53rd Street, a cluster of nineteenth-century tenements was left standing and architect Bruce Graham's multisided office building rose around and above them. Here a trompe l'oeil mural near the entrance on 53rd Street screens the old from the new.

32: *During the 1920s and 30s, countless New York buildings were modeled after Spanish castles or Italian villas, and topped with red ceramic tile roofs. Many of the buildings, and even more of the roofs, have disappeared —victims of redevelopment, deferred maintenance, and harsh weather.*

This is a photograph taken from the top of the MGM Building of one picturesque survivor, the Warwick Hotel on 54th Street.

By way of a postscript, these Spanish tiles have since been replaced by a more practical copper roof.

33: *In 1904, when Patrick Joseph Clarke from Co. Lei-
trim, Ireland, opened his saloon in a typical 1880s tene-
ment building on Third Avenue beneath the elevated
train, the prospect of its being preserved almost as an
historic shrine would never have occurred to him.*

*But in the 1960s, after the El had been torn down and
Third Avenue transformed, the developer of 919 Third
Avenue, between 53rd and 54th Streets, had to contend
with the preservationist attitude of the owners of P. J.
Clarke's and long negotiations finally resulted in a com-
promise. Tishman Realty was to acquire the building
with the proviso that it be leased back to the restaurant
owners for ninety-nine years.*

34–35: *At the southeast corner of 42nd Street and
Broadway stands a great old building that's been there
since 1902. Today it's an office building, but originally it
was the Hotel Knickerbocker, an important center of
New York's social and cultural life. Located as it was
just two blocks north of the old Metropolitan Opera
House, the Knickerbocker was the preferred residence
of Enrico Caruso, and he is said to have sung the "Star
Spangled Banner" from his window to the crowds assembled below in Times Square when the armistice was
announced in 1918.*

36–37: *A unique "double image" of midtown Manhattan as seen from and reflected in the surface of the IBM
Building, while it was still under construction in 1982.
At left, looking south down Madison Avenue, the out-
lines of the Chrysler, Pan Am, and still unfinished AT&T
buildings can be discerned. To the right, along 57th
Street, the curved facade of 9 West 57th Street, with the
Hudson River and New Jersey beyond: an impressive,
visual tour de force.*

38–39: *These flying buttresses seem worthy of a medieval cathedral, but in fact are purely decorative and form part of the ornate tower of architect Cass Gilbert's Woolworth Building at 233 Broadway, opposite City Hall Park. It was built in 1913 and immediately dubbed the "Cathedral of Commerce" in reference to its architecture and its builder, F.W. Woolworth of five-and-dime store fame. At 792 feet, the Woolworth Building was for many years the world's tallest building until the Chrysler Building was completed in 1930.*

This photograph was taken from the old observation deck, no longer accessible to the public. Recently restored to its original grandeur, the Woolworth Building —now dwarfed by the nearby World Trade Center— remains one of New York's great treasures.

40–41: *St. Patrick's Cathedral, begun in 1858 when Fifth Avenue and 50th Street was still a wilderness, was dedicated in 1879. Its architect James Renwick designed it in traditional Gothic style with a ground plan in the form of a Latin cross. This is readily apparent when viewed from above but not often realized from street level. Although St. Patrick's is among the twenty or so largest churches in the world, its size is strangely minimized by the truly enormous buildings surrounding it.*

42: *The footbridge connecting East 103rd Street in Manhattan with Ward's Island in the East River is one of several eye-catching spans around the city that have been painted in unusual, bright colors—in this case red, pink, and blue—rather than the typically dull grays and greens of most municipal structures.*

43: *For a brief time before 1931 when the Empire State Building superseded it, the Chrysler Building was the world's tallest structure at 1,048 feet.*

Its graceful tapering spire and splendid Art Deco detailing have earned it a special place in the affections of architectural enthusiasts and all New Yorkers. The architect William Van Alen made extensive use of metal ornamentation, including twelve huge gargoyles that project from the upper reaches of the tower, and which were modeled after the radiator caps on 1929 Chrysler cars.

"These have been photographed countless times, from almost every angle, but this is, as far as I know, the only one taken from directly overhead, thanks to the scaffold built to repair the top."

44, 45: "For almost two weeks in 1983 I covered for Time *magazine the re-creation of King Kong's famous ascent of the Empire State Building, this time as an inflatable balloon by Robert Keith & Co., makers of cold-air inflatables for advertising and show purposes.*

"Except for a few brief moments of glory, such as shown in the first photograph here, the project turned out to be an almost total fiasco. Bad weather, high winds, lack of experience, and just plain old bad luck defeated the best efforts of all those concerned.

"Even the most blasé New Yorkers felt sorry for the sponsors as the King Kong balloon hung limply from the tower and had to be content with fond memories of the 1930s film which started the whole thing."

46–47: *Unnoticed by most passersby, the name of the Empire State Building is proudly displayed in gilt intaglio above the main entrance on Fifth Avenue.*

48: *"While on assignment for a* Town & Country *maga-zine photographic essay on Manhattan, we flew over Harlem in a helicopter three thousand feet above the street. To our surprise a big jetliner flew right below us on its way into La Guardia Airport—just another of those instances where I was lucky to be in the right place at an opportune moment."*

49: "It's a bird, it's a plane, it's…Superman!" Or rather it's the Superman balloon in the annual Macy's Thanksgiving Day Parade, floating high above Broadway near Macy's Department Store at the end of its route. The parade is a magical event when everyone, no matter how old, becomes a child once again.

   Floats, balloons, celebrities, and bands change from year to year, but Superman remains a perennial favorite with the crowds.

50–51: When it was first laid out in 1858, the vast oasis of green in the middle of Manhattan was called "The Central Park" and in this photograph we see just how central it is. From 59th to 110th streets, from Fifth to

Eighth avenues, the park's eight hundred forty-three
acres of woods, lakes, lawns, and playing fields have
something for everyone.
  Frederick Law Olmsted, who—together with Calvert

Vaux—designed the park, was also the architect of Riverside Drive and Riverside Park, seen here along the
Hudson at the bottom of the photograph, and Morning-
side Park, which begins at the northwest corner of Cen-

tral Park and continues northward to join a narrow
ribbon of park land farther uptown.

*52–53, 54–55: Central Park clad in brilliant autumn
colors; somber winter garb (overleaf) is seen from high
up in the Majestic Apartments at Central Park West and
72nd Street.*

56, 57: *A few years ago, Len Silverfine, of the Big Idea Company, envisioned a plan to have the world's largest American flag made and to fly it from the Verrazano-Narrows Bridge as an appropriate companion to the Statue of Liberty in welcoming visitors entering New York Harbor. When the flag was finally a reality, it was displayed to the public first in Evansville, Indiana, and later was shown in Washington, D.C., and then in New York's Central Park to help raise funds for the project.*

The first photograph demonstrates the flag's enormous dimensions (compare it to the size of a typical city block along Central Park West); the second photograph, taken from closer in, shows the flag covering five softball diamonds.

Unfortunately, the money needed to bring the project to fruition was never raised and the flag was finally donated by the sponsors to the people of the United States.

58: *Rockefeller Center's original buildings of 1930–32 were designed by a consortium of three firms working together under the name Associated Architects. Their extensive use of ornamental sculpture on all the component units of the center was made possible through a combination of contemporary taste, architectural priorities, and Rockefeller sponsorship.*

In this 1982 photograph, workers are seen in the process of restoring one of the three enamel-and-metal plaques symbolic of Dance, Theater, and Song, sculpted by Hildreth Meiere, on the 50th Street side of Radio City Music Hall.

59: *High above Times Square the clock of the Paramount Building no longer marks the time for thousands of tourists and other passersby, and the huge theater at street level, where Frank Sinatra's voice once made teenagers swoon, is just a memory.*

The Paramount Building, on Broadway between 43rd and 44th streets, dates from 1926, although its Art Deco clock tower was added a few years later.

*60: Philip Johnson and John Burgee's AT&T Building at
Madison Avenue between 55th and 56th streets was completed in 1984 and has been called everything from a
"corporate highboy," to a "high-rise Chippendale
clock" because of its distinctive roofline.*

   *This is a view from the roof looking through the orbic-
ular opening at the center of the pediment, east toward
the Citicorp Building.*

61: *The north side of the AT&T Building from a perch above 56th Street. Various textured materials—granite, marble, concrete, and asphalt—are softened by the light dusting of snow.*

62–63: *Artist José de Creeft's huge bronze sculpture of Alice in Wonderland has been a favorite gathering place for children in Central Park since 1959. Here we see* *Alice and her friends from a rather unusual spot— directly overhead.*

64: *"Photographing the globe in the lobby of the Daily News Building at 42nd Street and Second Avenue turned out to be a big production. In order to get the right effect I waited until late in the evening when the usually busy lobby is quiet; then I crawled out over the ceiling and aimed the camera directly down at the globe. By then the lobby was totally deserted so my assistant went out and rounded up some students to stand near the globe.*

"The entire project took a lot of time and trouble but my assistants that evening—Mark Mittleman and Dith Pran—were terrific. Dith Pran's heroic adventures in Cambodia have been retold in the film The Killing Fields."

65: *One of New York's most impressive, famous, and busy public spaces: the main concourse of Grand Central Terminal, seen in this photograph from one hundred twenty-five feet above the floor. Grand Central (it's a terminal, not a station) was built in 1913 and its architects, Warren & Wetmore, produced a masterful blending of utility and grandeur.*

66: *Thousands of revelers gather in Times Square each year to watch the electric "ball" drop and usher in the New Year.*

The intersection of Seventh Avenue and Broadway was formerly known as Longacre Square; it only became Times Square when the New York Times newspaper company moved its building to 42nd Street in 1904.

67: *A closer look at New Year's Eve celebrants. They seem to float on a river of gold, although it's actually the reflection of electric signs in the rain-slicked street.*

68–69: *"On the day the U.S. athletes from the 1984 Los Angeles Olympic Games were accorded a great welcome to New York City, I was ensconced high up on the Woolworth Building, overlooking lower Broadway and City Hall, a perfect spot from which to photograph the parade and the official welcoming ceremonies.*

"A New York ticker tape parade is an incomparable experience, and especially so for me from my perch above the blizzard of paper, surrounded by the towers of lower Manhattan, and with downtown Brooklyn off in the distance beyond the bridge."

70: *A close-up view of the parade, as the Olympic winners and their police escorts march north on Broadway. Today's version of the ticker tape parade involves more familiar forms of shredded paper than the original material, long since rendered obsolete by typewriters and computers. The festive atmosphere, however, is still the same.*

71: *Each fall the New York City Marathon begins at the Staten Island end of the Verrazano-Narrows Bridge, and ends in Central Park after the runners follow a route through Brooklyn, Queens, and the Bronx. The bridge itself is a magnificent sight, and at 6,690 feet surpassed in 1964 the Golden Gate Bridge in San Francisco to become the world's longest.*

"In 1981, I was all set to climb on the cables at the Brooklyn end of the bridge, when gale-force winds at the top caused Dave Baxley, the public relations spokesman for the Triborough Bridge & Tunnel Authority, to issue strict orders to the press: no photographers allowed due to hazardous conditions.

"Luckily, he made an exception in my case—I already had my permit and safety equipment—but it was the most terrifying ascent I've ever experienced."

72–73: *In the early nineteenth century, South Street, on the East River, was an incredibly busy place where sailing vessels from all over the world docked to load and unload their cargoes. Its importance was supplanted when the big steam-powered ships, which required deeper moorings, moved to the piers along the Hudson River. A long period of decline and decay began at South Street, which has been reversed in recent years. Now it's a center for entertainment, excursions, and dining.*

In 1983 the grand opening of the South Street Seaport complex, developed by the Rouse Corporation with the Seaport Museum, took place in the vast open square at the foot of Fulton Street. Musicians, jugglers, clowns, speeches, champagne, and balloons—thousands of them —marked the occasion.

74–75: *Early morning, the streets of lower Manhattan in 1982: thousands of bicyclists wearing identical orange Day-Glow vests are about to start on a citywide bike-athon through the five boroughs of New York, under the sponsorship of Citibank and American Youth Hostels.*

76: On Thanksgiving Day the New-York Historical
Society at Central Park West and 77th Street is where
the Macy's parade starts each year. On the right is a
tower of the San Remo Apartments, between 74th and
75th streets.

77: This monochromatic view of the Empire State
Building's distinctive top wasn't the result of an especially vivid sunset. Instead it resulted from a trip up
the tower during the Christmas season, when the skyscraper was illuminated with the holiday colors of green
and red.

   The mast that crowns the Empire State was originally
intended to be used as a mooring place for dirigibles,
but the location and height made it impractical for this
purpose.

78: One of the enormous metal fins on the mast of the
Empire State Building, photographed just after sunset.

   Rising some 1,250 feet above Fifth Avenue at 34th
Street, the Empire State was recognized for thirty years
as the world's tallest building. Designed by Shreve, Lamb
& Harmon, it was built in 1930–31 on land where the
Astor mansions had once stood and where the Waldorf-
Astoria Hotel had been located from 1893 to 1929.

79: The graceful tapering outline of the top of the
Chrysler Building, showing the special lights installed
during the restoration of the tower. The building's owner
Jack Kent Cooke was determined to revive all the original splendor of this landmark, including the lamps
framing the triangular windows in the curved upper
stories.

80: "One night I was camped out on Liberty Island so I'd be able to take some good sunrise photographs of the statue. I happened to glance northward and almost couldn't believe my eyes. Miles away, right beside the Empire State Building, was a huge bottle, lit up and suspended in midair.

"I later found out that it was a publicity stunt for Cordoniu sparkling wine, and in this photograph both the helicopter holding the bottle and the helicopter holding the photographer recording the event for his client are visible."

81: Two of Manhattan's most stately and celebrated grandes dames, *the Empire State Building and the Chrysler Building, photographed from atop the Queensboro Bridge at sunrise.*

Each of these was once the world's tallest building, but even though this distinction has been lost, they continue to hold our attention—two dowager queens of great power and beauty.

82–83: In this photograph, made at dusk from the top of the Williamsburg Bridge, are the brilliantly illuminated towers of three famous landmarks: the 1926 clock tower of the Consolidated Edison Company, on Irving Place and 14th Street; the campanile tower of the Metropolitan Life Insurance Company's building at Madison Avenue and 23rd Street, put up in 1909; and the Empire State Building, just beyond to the north.

84–85: *A panorama of downtown Manhattan from the top of the Brooklyn tower of the Williamsburg Bridge.*

With a span of 1,600 feet, the Williamsburg Bridge is slightly longer and higher than the Brooklyn Bridge. Since 1903 it has carried horsecars, pushcarts, cars, trucks, subway trains, and pedestrians from Delancey Street on the Lower East Side to Broadway in Brooklyn.

86: *A laser beam light show, presented in May 1981, to celebrate the fiftieth anniversary of the Empire State Building.*

"Laser photography can be very difficult, so our preparations were even more elaborate and careful than usual. Three locations were scouted and reserved from which we could see and photograph the show. This shot was made from atop the RCA Building in Rockefeller Center, looking due south at an unforgettable event."

87: *The twin towers of the World Trade Center are visible for miles around and have a prominent, even overwhelming, place in the city skyline. At 110 stories they are New York's tallest buildings, and from being originally reviled they have come to be accepted and even grudgingly admired. Minoru Yamasaki & Associates, with Emery Roth & Sons, were the architects of the World Trade Center's towers, owned by the Port Authority of New York and New Jersey. Construction began in 1962 and continued for several years.*

"In order to photograph the first light of dawn reflected in the towers' windows, my assistant and I scrambled to the top of the Manhattan Bridge in a record four-and-a-half minutes (it usually takes us more like ten) so that we'd get the light of the sun and the setting moon together."

88–89: *When this photograph was taken in 1981, New York City's television stations still broadcast their signals from the top of the Empire State Building (now they use the World Trade Center). The red lamps, which indicate the antenna, were regularly inspected between one and four o'clock in the morning.*

"Here, on a particularly chilly September morning—my birthday—I was given permission to climb to the top of the antenna. It was bitter cold and because I had on a lot of heavy clothes I could only climb to the second tier. That's where I photographed this maintenance man 're-lamping,' as they say in the trade, although most of us would say 'changing bulbs.'"

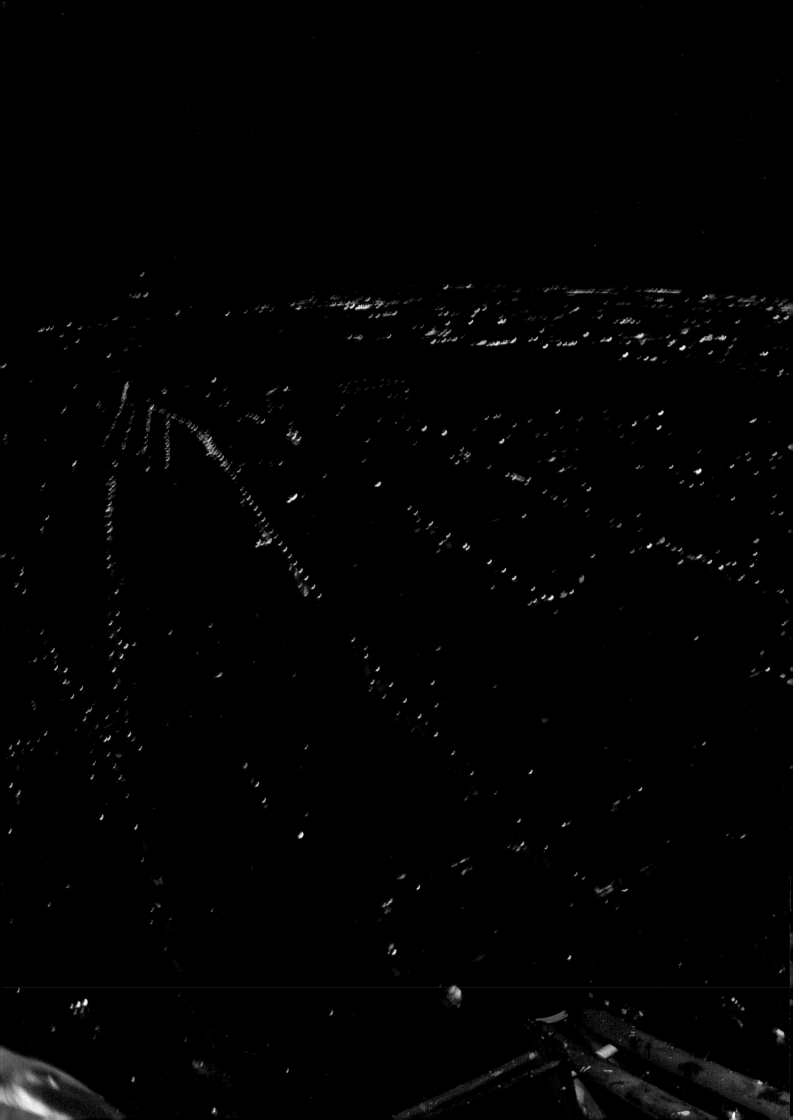

90–91: *At the 104th floor level of the Empire State Building, a worker kneels on the ice shield that projects out over the side of the tower, rigging the hoist used to raise the King Kong balloon (see pages 44–45).*

The time is just after sunset, with the lights of New Jersey visible across the Hudson River.

92–93: *An ironworker gingerly making his way along a girder during construction of Trump Tower in 1983, some six hundred feet above the ground.*

The sixty-eight-story Trump Tower, containing shops, offices, and condominium apartments, is higher than zoning would normally permit on its ground area, but its developer was able to exceed the usual limit by purchasing the air rights above Tiffany's and Bonwit Teller's which adjoin on 57th Street.

94–95: *The workmen sheathing the roof of the AT&T Building seem oblivious to the danger of working so high up.*

In the background is the unique silhouette of the Citicorp Building, with its sloped roof designed to capture solar heat during the energy crisis of the mid-1970s, but now falling into the same category as the Empire State Building's dirigible mooring mast: more practical on the drawing board than in reality.

Hugh Stubbins & Associates were the architects of the Citicorp Center at Lexington Avenue and 53rd Street, a complex which sparked the recent slew of corporate office towers east of Park Avenue built in the past ten years.

96: *Everyone is familiar with the famous pair of lions, dubbed Patience and Fortitude, guarding the entrance to the New York Public Library at 42nd Street and Fifth Avenue, but this view is of the less decorative though certainly more protective roof of the seventy-five-year-old building.*

Looking east the camera confronts some high-rise neighbors, including the Chrysler Building, the stark black-and-white form of 489 Fifth Avenue, and the eclectic tower of 8-10 East 40th Street.

97: *Looking down from the north tower of the World Trade Center, toward the plaza 110 floors below, surrounded by the excavations and construction work for the other buildings of the Port Authority's gargantuan complex in 1974 when this photograph was made. From here the sleek aluminum spandrels, which enclose almost ten million feet of office space, can be seen in their plain and fancy variations.*

98: *A tale of two cities, or perhaps two eras.*

In the foreground, the snow-covered low-rise buildings of the Brooklyn waterfront are reminiscent of a turn-of-the-century painting by one of the Ashcan School artists—Luks or Sloan—while across the East River the towers of later generations bring us right up to our own time.

"On the cold morning this photograph was taken I was in a helicopter, where it was even colder than down on the ground. I almost lost my fingers to frostbite. The early morning hour explains the serenity of the streets and the absence of traffic on the Brooklyn Bridge."

99: *This photograph taken from the top of the AT&T Building records the intersection of Fifth Avenue and 57th Street during construction of Trump Tower. Notable neighbors include the Crown Building with its pointed green roof; the black and white monolith at 9 West 57th Street built by Sheldon Solow in 1972, and designed by Skidmore, Owings & Merrill; the Plaza Hotel, a landmark by Henry Hardenbergh that has defined the square at Fifth Avenue and Central Park South since 1907; and the stately white office building at 745 Fifth Avenue, designed by Ely Jacques Kahn in 1930 and originally known as the Squibb Building.*

100: *Now here's a room with a view—and air-conditioned at that. It's the crane operator's cab on the top of the Trump Tower during its construction. Cranes of enormous size like this, which rise as the building does, have become the major components of modern high-rise construction in recent years.*

Off to the left the steel skeleton of the AT&T Building gives an indication of its final form.

101: *During the restoration project initiated by its new owners, many of the Crown Building's architectural details were lavishly gilded (see page 17).*

"I happened to be up on the scaffolding on the day that a workman added his own final touches of gold leaf to a bas-relief on the tower. Who would have thought that in 1920 an anonymous stone carver was so concerned with providing anatomical detail on a mythical beast, so high up out of everyone's view?"

102: *An artisan applies sealant prior to gold-leafing one of the sculptural details on the Helmsley Building at 230 Park Avenue. He is just one of what sometimes seems to be a small army of skilled craftsmen who ply their trades high above the city, invisible to the pedestrians who hurry by each day.*

The spectacular gold leaf decoration of what had

originally been the New York Central Building was done
at the behest of developer Harry Helmsley who acquired
the building some sixty years after it was completed
in 1929.

Warren & Wetmore were the architects of this grandi-
ose structure that straddles Park Avenue at 45th Street,
and which was designed to serve as the headquarters of
the then-thriving New York Central Railroad.

103: A workman cleaning one of the elaborate stone
finials on the cross above St. Patrick's Cathedral's main
entrance on Fifth Avenue, during the restoration project that was completed in 1979.

"My hand is visible in the picture, just below the
workman. I'm holding the camera support and down
below is another photographer who was assigned to do
a story on me."

104–105: "One morning in 1979 I set out to photograph from the top of the World Trade Center only to discover when I got there and looked up from the street that the tops of the towers were enveloped in clouds. Rather than turn around and go home, I decided to see what the crew did on bad days, so I checked in by telephone with the men at the top installing the new television antenna on the north tower.

"They told me to come up anyway and when I arrived on the roof I knew why. There below us was the magnificent spire of the Woolworth Building pointing up through the mist. It was a great feeling to think that here I was on top of New York's highest building, shooting the Woolworth, which, fifty years ago, had once been New York's highest building."

106–107: The effects of severe weather—especially lightning—had caused widespread deterioration to the metal sheathing at the top of the Chrysler Building. When workmen from the Brisk Waterproofing Company finished their restoration project on the uppermost reaches of the tower, they celebrated by "topping-off" the scaffolding—a rite that workers have conducted since medieval times to mark completion of a roof structure.

"The man near the top of the flag is Mike Radigan, foreman of the crew. Mike and I have been good friends ever since our days spent together during the restoration of the Chrysler Building."

108–109: After local television stations began transmitting their signals from the new antenna on the top of one of the World Trade Center's towers, the precarious project of dismantling the old antenna atop the Empire State Building was undertaken by the North American Tower Company of Pittman, New Jersey.

Here one of that firm's amazingly agile workers, Mark Frates, ascends to the top, with the help of a fellow worker who's even higher up on the mast, and who can just be made out in the reflective sunglasses of this man.

"These guys are fearless. There's no margin for error in their jobs as they 'kiss steel,' climbing around on little batwing supports, held only by a rope lifeline!"

110–11: The Queensboro Bridge, linking 59th Street in Manhattan with Long Island City in Queens, was completed in 1909. When the architect saw the finished span for the first time he's said to have exclaimed, "My God, it's a blacksmith's shop!" referring to the intricate network of steel which characterizes the bridge.

The two middle support towers of the four thousand foot-long suspension bridge arise from Roosevelt Island. In this photograph the southern tip of the island is not unlike a mammoth version of the Seine's Ile de la Cité in Paris.

"In 1978, when the bridge was being repainted, I spent several frustrating weeks trying to cut through the red tape and get permission from the city to photograph the work in progress. I finally received the necessary permits and went straight to the top, my first climb to the uppermost reaches of the bridge. There I found Angelo Begonia happily slathering a rust-preventive undercoat onto one of the towers."

112: One of Manhattan's more exotic means of public transportation is the Roosevelt Island Tram. For the price of a subway token a traveler can quietly soar above the East River in a genuine Swiss cable car, from 59th Street and Second Avenue to the apartment houses and municipal hospitals on Roosevelt Island, enjoying sweeping views of Sutton Place, the Queensboro Bridge, and the flat expanse of Long Island's western end.

Originally intended as a temporary measure built to serve the commuters who live on Roosevelt Island until a subway tunnel was completed, the tram now appears to be a permanent institution.

113: In a 1982 photograph, steelworkers go about their job high up on the framework of the AT&T Building. At left the red roofs of the Ritz Tower underscore the more austere architecture of its next-door neighbor, The Galleria.

114–15: During the summer of 1983 the Brooklyn Bridge was specially illuminated to honor its one-hundredth anniversary. Here, in this photograph taken from the top of the east tower, the lights of Manhattan sparkle in the distance, and the great arched stone towers and graceful steel cables are bathed in a centennial red glow.

The Great East River Suspension Bridge, as it was then called, was designed by John A. Roebling, in 1867. However, construction began under the supervision of his son Washington A. Roebling. When first opened to the public in May 1883, pedestrians were charged a toll of one cent. Today it's free, and the Brooklyn Bridge is still as magnificent a sight as the day it was finished—a marvel of engineering and civic pride.

116: The Brooklyn Bridge has probably inspired more paintings, photographs, anecdotes, legends, swindles, and jokes than any other in the world.

Photographed just after sundown the tall pointed arches seem to float in midair, although they rise two hundred seventy-two feet above the East River and are built of enormous granite blocks.

Until the completion of the Williamsburg Bridge in 1903, this was the world's longest suspension bridge, with a span of approximately sixteen hundred feet and a total length of six thousand feet.

Just barely discernible beyond the bridge are City Hall, the Tweed Courthouse, and the Municipal Building.

117: "One fine Sunday afternoon during the summer of 1981, we climbed to the top of the Brooklyn Bridge to enjoy music rising from an open-air concert at the South Street Seaport. Soon the scene below was transformed into Venice magnified a hundredfold."

118: *From the east tower of the Brooklyn Bridge this photograph shows the Manhattan Bridge, built in 1909 to connect Canal Street in Manhattan with Flatbush Avenue in Brooklyn. The engineer who designed the span was Gustav Lindenthal, responsible also for the Hell Gate and Queensboro bridges.*

"A sudden shower at the end of a clear, crisp, autumn day provided the opportunity for this photograph with its dramatic cloud effects in the western sky."

119: *"On June 28, 1982, my assistant, John Kidd, and I were at the top of the Brooklyn Bridge photographing Brooklyn Heights. While waiting for the daylight to change we laid down to sun bathe, but fell asleep. When we woke up we were disoriented because all around us there was an eerie stillness. I felt as though the "bomb" had dropped. We peered down to the roadbed, one hundred thirty-five feet below us, and saw there were no cars or pedestrians on the bridge, no noise... nothing. We were mystified and found out when we climbed down that a cable had snapped, killing a tourist in a freak accident and thus causing the bridge to be completely closed down for several hours.*

"This photograph records that most unusual scene—

the Brooklyn Bridge, probably for the first time in a century, totally empty."

120: *"One day in August of 1983, I got a call from George Zambelli of the Zambelli Fireworks Company alerting me to a private display of pyrotechnics scheduled for that very evening. The occasion was a birthday celebration for industrialist H. J. Heinz, and his family had been given permission to launch fireworks from a barge anchored in the East River, opposite their Sutton Place residence, as a climax to the party.*

"Somehow the arrangements had been kept totally secret to prevent crowds of curious New Yorkers from jamming the nearby streets and the F.D.R. Drive. Naturally, when the noise of exploding rockets echoed through the Upper East Side, residents thought the revolution had begun! I was perched on the top of the Queensboro Bridge photographing this once-in-a-lifetime event: a Zambelli fireworks spectacular with me as the unofficial photographer of record."

122: *Peter B. Kaplan on a batwing support atop the Empire State Building. Photo by Aziz Rahman © 1984 Peter B. Kaplan*

TECHNICAL NOTES

The Pole Photo

The photographs on pages 26, 36–37, 46–47, 50–51, 56, 58, 59, 71, 97, 103, and 106–107 were made with the devices and techniques developed by Peter B. Kaplan to take close-up pictures of tall buildings without the necessity of using a helicopter, which can't get as close as is sometimes required. The resulting picture has a wide-angle feeling, and gives the photographer a sense of rapport between camera and subject as seen on pages 106–107. Consisting, basically, of a special lightweight camera affixed to the end of a collapsible metal pole, the device used for taking "pole" shots of buildings began as an ordinary tripod, with a 35 mm camera attached, held out over the top and side of a building. This was in 1974, when the photographer was attempting to take some new and unusual pictures of the World Trade Center's towers (see page 97). The initial results of these experiments led Peter B. Kaplan to work on refining the technique and, with the advice and help of Marty Forscher, of Professional Camera Repair Service, Inc., at 37 West 47th Street, New York City, building an improved version of the original extension pole, using lightweight, collapsible poles and a normal 35mm fully automatic camera with a motor drive, but with its batteries removed. A special battery with a 35-foot cord attached both gives power to and triggers the camera.

When the pole is extended seventeen feet or less, Peter B. Kaplan is able to hold it by himself, and an assistant triggers the camera. For more difficult setups, a special pole may be extended to a length of forty feet (see page 26 for an example of a twenty-seven-foot pole photo). A second assistant must help to steady the camera and pole in order to aim it properly.

Often, because of the angle of the sun or the pecu-

59

71

97

26

liarities of the building being photographed, the actual pole and camera, or their shadows, appear in the final picture (see pages 46–47, 103, and 106–107).

Perhaps the most spectacular of all the pole shots, as developed by Peter B. Kaplan, is that taken from the top of the IBM building with a highly reflective facade, where a mirror image of the surrounding area produces startling effects (see pages 36–37).

The Cherry-Picker Photo

Several photographs in this book were taken from the vantage point of a cherry picker, the name used to describe a large, mobile crane with an easily maneuverable boom topped by a small work platform. It is the type of crane often used by repairmen for public utility companies who must clear away branches from and work on high tension wires. By using a cherry picker, the photographer can get close enough in to the subject for detail, but at the same time keep enough distance to allow other objects or some of the surrounding area into the image. In short, what the pole shot is to the top of a building, the cherry-picker shot is to the trees, water, traffic, or lower stories of a building. A cherry picker can extend as high as 150 feet (about fifteen stories). Whereas in a pole shot the photographer and camera are apart, in a cherry-picker shot the photographer has the camera in his hand as he rides in the bucket of the cherry picker, and so can fully control the picture. For examples of the cherry-picker shots, see pages 31, 33, 34–35, 57, 61, and 62–63.

The Fish-eye Lens Photo

Photographs in this book taken with a full-frame

46–47

103

106–107

36–37

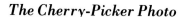
31

33

34–35

57

61

62–63

24–25.

45

1

0–51

56

58

60.

64

65

8–69

90–91

100

10–111

114–115

128

fish-eye lens, (a super wide-angle lens), are those reproduced on pages 1, 24–25, 36–37, 45, 46–47, 50–51, 56, 57, 58, 60, 64, 65, 68–69, 90–91, 100, 103, 106–107, 110–111, 114–115, and 128.

The fish-eye lens is a little understood lens. With many years of experimentation—and due to the restriction of "height photography"—Peter B. Kaplan has learned to "distort" the distortion in order to compensate and correct the natural fish-eye curve. Sometimes, the photographer lets the curve appear across the frame to create the feeling of height and range, as though it were seen from outer space.

The Gyroscope

The gyroscope is an expensive but invaluable tool used in situations when the camera platform is too unstable for a tripod, such as on a boat, in a helicopter, or on a swaying bridge cable. The gyroscope also permits the photographer to shoot with a wide open lens and slow shutter speeds in low-light conditions and to maintain depth of field. See page 79.

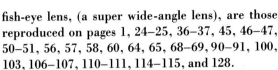

79

The Remote Control Photo

The remote offers great flexibility for the photographer in any number of circumstances: for reasons of press restrictions; danger of life; or when the photographer's presence would be intrusive in recording an event, but when the desired camera position is somewhere the photographer can't be himself. There are three ways of making a remote picture: hard wire; radio signal; and infrared. For example, in the photo on pages 18–19, Mr. Kaplan can be seen 120 feet below where he is firing his remote via infrared sensor.

18–19

125

8

29

30

43

44

67

70

74–75

81

116

The Long Lens Photo

Very often a photographer can achieve the special effect he is striving for only by using powerful telephoto lenses to make compressed land or cityscape views bringing together the foreground and background. See pages 8, 29, 30, 43, 44, 62–63, 67, 70, 74–75, 81, and 116 for examples of these long shots.

The photograph on page 80 was made with a 600 mm lens plus two telescopic extenders, amounting to a total of 1700 mm, in order to capture the details of an event taking place some five and a half miles away.

80

78

Other Remarks

When new lighting was installed on the top of the Empire State Building in 1978 (see page 78), the color temperature of the lamps had been balanced for tungsten light with the result that the silver-toned aluminum fins on the mast appear gold-colored when photographed on Kodachrome film balanced for daylight. Since then the lamps have been replaced and are now balanced for daylight film, so photographs taken now show the fins in their real color.

The managers of the Empire State Building, after an initial period of skepticism about Peter B. Kaplan's plan to climb up to the top and extend poles over the side of the tower, have been extremely cooperative in helping the photographer to experiment and shoot from the top of this landmark. In what must surely be regarded as a "first" for the building, Peter B. Kaplan and his wife, Sharon Rosenbush, were married at the top of the Empire State Building in May 1985.

BIBLIOGRAPHY

Alpern, Andrew, and Seymour Durst. *Holdouts!* New York: McGraw-Hill, 1984.

Federal Writers Project. *The WPA Guide to New York City.* New York: Pantheon Books, 1982.

Goldberger, Paul. *The City Observed, New York: A Guide to the Architecture of Manhattan.* New York: Vintage Books, 1979.

Norton, Thomas E., and Jerry E. Patterson. *Living It Up: A Guide to the Named Apartment Houses of New York.* New York: Atheneum, 1984.

Rosen, Laura. *Top of the City, New York's Hidden Rooftop World.* New York: Thames & Hudson, 1982.

Tauranac, John. *Essential New York.* New York: Holt, Rinehart & Winston, 1979.

White, Norval, and Elliot Willensky. *AIA Guide to New York City.* rev. ed., New York: Collier Books, 1978.

Wurman, Richard Saul. *NYC Access.* Los Angeles: Accesspress, 1983.

ACKNOWLEDGMENTS

There are many people and organizations, both behind-the-scenes and directly involved with me, whose invaluable help has made these photographs possible.

With special thanks to: the Archdiocese of New York; Blakley Tree Co., Inc.; David Baxley; Brinx Coatings, Inc.; Brisk Waterproofing Co. Inc.; Jack Kent Cooke; Fireworks by Grucci; Charles Giugno; HRH Construction Corp.; Mr. and Mrs. Harry Helmsley; IBM Public Relations Office; Island Helicopter; Don Kaplan; Robert Keith & Co. (San Diego, Ca.); Kodiak Crane Co.; Lime Waterproofing, Inc.; the Mayor's Office of Film, Theater & Broadcasting; New York City Parks Commission; the New-York Historical Society; the New York Police Department Movie & TV Unit; Newmark & Co. Real Estate, Inc.; One Times Square Building; the Police Commissioner of New York City and staff; Lee Pomerance; the Port Authority of New York & New Jersey; Professional Camera Repair; Michael B. Radigan; Remco Group; Rockefeller Center Public Relations staff;

128: "An image that needs no introduction and almost no explanation since it's become so well known. The photograph I call Moon Over Manhattan was taken in 1979 at the top of the television antenna being installed on the World Trade Center. It features Dick Reilly, with a supporting cast of his co-workers."

Howard Rubenstein & Associates; Ruth Sarfaty; Science Faction Corp.; Len Silverfine Productions; Special Operations Division; Joyce Starvis; Statue of Liberty-Ellis Island Foundation, Inc.; Ben Strauss Industries, Inc.; Bill Suchaneck; Robert Tinker; Triborough Bridge & Tunnel Authority; Trump Organization, Inc.; Universal Builders Supply, Inc.; William A. White/Tishman East, Inc.; Woolworth Building Management; Tom Young; and Zambelli Fireworks Mfg. Co., Inc.

To my clients, many thanks: Michael Abramson & Associates, Inc.; *America* magazine; *Dialogue* magazine; Empire State Building; Ford-Fyffe & Co.; Hudson-Shatz Painting Co., Inc.; the Douglas Leigh Organization; *Life* magazine; J.P. Lohman; Minskoff Organization, Inc.; *New York* magazine; the *New York Times Magazine*; *Newsweek* magazine; *Time* magazine; *Town & Country* magazine; and Wells, Rich, Greene, Inc.

And to my friends and assistants for their devotion and skills: Harriet Avramescu; Barbara Baumann; Barbara Bohrer; Steve Bornes; Stephen R. Brown; Todd Bryant; Eric S. Cohen; Lara Donin; Stephan Findel; Eddie Fleshner; Joel Gordon; J. Stephen Hall; John Herndon; John Kidd; Mark A. Mittleman; Roy Morsch; Willie Nugent; Mitch Penna; Dith Pran; Michael C. Radigan, Jr.; Aziz Rahman; Peter Schaffer; Eric Schnakenberg; Charles O. Slavens; Barbara Strauss; Sarah Todd; Norman Tomlin; Amanda Vaskas; Steven Weingrad; David Wills; Jan Worthington; and Jerry Young.

To those responsible for the myriad details of assembling this book: Theodore Kaplan; Bob Di Giacomo, Janice Lipzin, and Caryl Wendkos-La Torre in my studio; and Bob Morton, Ruth Peltason, and Dirk Luykx at Harry N. Abrams Publishers.

Plus the hundreds of courageous men who work "high on New York".... Thank you.

—Peter B. Kaplan